Weapons & Warfare

Weapons & Warfare

From the Stone Age to the Space Age

Milton Meltzer

Illustrated by
Sergio Martinez

HarperCollins*Publishers*

Weapons & Warfare

From the Stone Age to the Space Age

Printed in the United States of America. For information address HarperCollins Children's Books, a division of HarperCollins Publishers, 10 East 53rd Street, New York, NY 10022.

Library of Congress Cataloging-in-Publication Data
Meltzer, Milton, date.
Weapons & warfare : from the stone age to the space age / by Milton Meltzer; illustrations by Sergio Martinez.
p. cm.
Includes bibliographical references and index.
Summary: Highlights some weapons of war explaining how and why they were developed, various responses people have had to them, and the impact they have had upon society.
ISBN 0-06-024875-0. — ISBN 0-06-024876-9 (lib. bdg.)
1. Weapons—Juvenile literature. 2. Military art and science—Juvenile literature. [1. Weapons. 2. Military art and science.] I. Martinez, Sergio, date. ill. II. Title.
U800.M34 1996 95-48464
355.02—dc20 CIP
AC

Typography by Tom Starace

7 8 9 10

❖

For Ben and Zack
in the hope they will
never have to bear arms

Contents

Foreword

Weapons and war, like everything else, have their social history. A book about them does not imply approval of combat or killing.

But weapons affect the lives of people who make them and use them—and, obviously, the lives of people against whom they are used.

Since weapons have been common for many thousands of years, it is worth looking into how and why they developed, and the impact they have had upon society.

This book is by no means a comprehensive treatment. To write about all weapons would take a huge encyclopedia. There are such studies, and this book's bibliography lists some of them. I chose to look at what interested me—how certain weapons came about, why they were adopted, and what some of the responses to them have been.

Technical aspects of weaponry are not explored in great detail. Again, such matters are fully covered in works devoted to military science and invention.

This is a book to browse through as you wish. For readers who have an interest in specific weapons, the index will prove a useful guide.

1 *How Did It Start?*

Who makes war?

You could answer, who doesn't?

Making war has been one of humankind's chief activities for thousands of years. Combat probably first occurred when groups of men in the Old Stone Age (before 10,000 B.C.) used crude stone weapons to fight with other groups over food, women, or land.

Archeologists digging down into the layers of prehistoric communities in the Middle East have found evidence that New Stone Age people were waging war as far back as 7000 B.C.

As the population grew in the earliest human societies, the local supply of food diminished. People were forced to migrate in search of food. Group competed with group for subsistence. Early warfare probably developed because of the competition for adequate food, and the tools used for hunting—the club, the spear, the knife—became the weapons of war.

In the thousands of years that followed before people began to record their history, no doubt other drives—such as the urge to dominate or the desire for independence—became additional causes of conflict.

2 *Club, Spear, Sling, and Bow*

The wooden club was the first true weapon fashioned during the Old Stone Age, that immense expanse of geologic time stretching back before 10,000 B.C. Primitive man made clubs by breaking off branches of trees or tearing stumps out of the ground. The club was a personal weapon, one that could be used to settle a dispute. Or to force a neighbor from a desirable cave, or to win a more attractive mate. Useful though it was, the club could be effective only close up, when the enemy (or animal) was within arm's reach. So to gain a greater striking distance, man developed the spear for throwing, the sling for hurling stones, and the bow for shooting arrows.

The earliest spears were wooden shafts, their points hardened by fire. Arrows too were wooden shafts, but smaller, with feathers and barbs added. These new weapons, which made it easier for Stone Age people to hunt animals, also were effective on other humans.

Over time man learned to chip stones to get a good cutting edge. Early craftsmen learned to lash flint and other sharp stones to wooden handles, using animal tendons and strips of rawhide. Out of this innovation came the stone club, the stone-tipped spear, and the flint arrowhead. It was with such primitive weapons as these that war was first fought. Of course, these weapons limited the harm people could do to each other in battle, for they could be used only at fairly close range, compared to weapons that would follow thousands of years later.

Wooden club

3 *Longbow and Crossbow*

An arrow shot from a bow has more power than a stone hurled from a sling, and can travel much farther. Native Americans have been known to shoot arrows straight through buffaloes. Prehistoric bows have been unearthed in Switzerland, and cave paintings show them in use. One of the most ancient of weapons, the bow goes back many thousands of years to the New Stone Age.

What bows and arrows were made of depended upon what was at hand. North American bows were made of hickory or ash—flexible woods that could be made to bend slightly in the center—with a cord stretched tightly from one end to the other.

Arrows were a smoothed shaft of wood with a pointed, barbed head at one end, and feathers attached to the other end for steadiness in flight. The heads of primitive arrows were usually made of flint or bone. Archers hold the arrow by one hand at the center of the bow and pull the cord back to the chest with the other hand, to obtain the greatest amount of tension. When the bowstring is released, the bow regains its shape and shoots the arrow toward its target.

Perhaps around 1000 B.C. the composite bow was invented by the Chaldeans in Mesopotamia (the area in modern-day Iraq between the Tigris and Euphrates rivers). Makers of the composite bow used three different materials: wood, split horn, and dried animal tendons. Small bows, they rarely exceeded four feet in length. But their power was astounding. An arrow flight of over 900 yards has been recorded with the composite bow. Soon its use extended all through Asia because it proved to be the most powerful kind of hand bow. Not until guns were invented did the composite bow fall out of use.

The bow was used in many parts of the ancient world. The Egyptians made them, even though wood was scarce in their land. The Greeks were good archers, too, although they used arrows mostly for hunting, and rarely in battle. Six-foot bows—longbows—were known to both the Egyptians and, thousands of years later, the Vikings.

The English in medieval times had bows the height of the average man, but some were longer than six feet. It took about a hundred pounds of pressure to draw a bow of this size. English bows were made mostly of yew. Because bows had become so essential in warfare, English kings encouraged archery by conducting competitions and awarding prizes to the winners. French rulers, on the other hand, were leery of the bow. They feared that if placed in the serfs' hands, they might be used in revolt.

Always on the lookout for greater power in weaponry, European soldiers of the fourteenth century began to experiment with a weapon new to them. It was the crossbow, a small, very stiff bow set crosswise at the end of a staff or stock. When its trigger was released, the crossbow's mechanism discharged a heavy bolt, propelling a short, sharp arrow with tremendous force.

The crossbow was developed by the Chinese long before Europeans created their own version of this weapon. (The crossbow has been found in Chinese tombs of the fourth century B.C.) Crossbows did not appear in Europe until much later. Gradually the crossbow won greater use on the battlefield because the power of its bolt was strong enough to penetrate armor at both short and medium range.

The crossbow was clumsier and had a slower rate of fire than the traditional bow. But the metal bolts or arrows shot from these machines flew farther and faster and more accurately than arrows of the conventional bow. Crossbows made their great mark in military history when the Norman army used them to defeat the Saxons in the Battle of Hastings in 1066.

The crossbow was frowned upon by some European aristocrats. In their view, fighting at a distance with missiles was beneath them. They clung to the tradition of their forefathers, which esteemed face-to-face combat. Pierre Bayard (c. 1474–1524), a French military hero who commanded in several important battles, had enemy crossbowmen executed when taken prisoner. The reason? Their weapon was a cowardly one, he thought, and their behavior treacherous. To kill the enemy from a distance without placing yourself in danger was not the behavior of a true knight.

Stone bow or prod

Testimony to the effectiveness of the crossbow was a Vatican edict of 1139. The bow was outlawed as being too barbarous for use in warfare between Christians. Firing it against Muslims or other infidels, however, was declared perfectly acceptable. Not every soldier respected the edict.

4 *Bronze Age to Iron Age*

Copper was the first nonprecious metal that man learned how to work. It is found in big and almost pure ingots in a natural state. But copper is not effective for military use. Body armor made of it can be easily pierced, and copper shaped into a weapon quickly loses its edge. But when it was found that intense heat could melt metals, craftsmen developed the technique of combining copper with scarce tin to produce hard bronze—the metal of conquerors.

The Bronze Age—roughly 2500–1000 B.C.—introduced a new chapter in weaponry. Bronze can be cast into any shape desired by using molds. This process led to a simpler way of making spearheads, arrowheads, and battle-axes. Bronze knife blades became longer and narrower and developed into a new weapon—the sword.

What the Bronze Age had introduced, the Iron Age, which began about 1000 B.C., improved upon. Iron was even stronger and harder than bronze, better suited to military needs. It is not scarce, and is widely distributed. Artisans learned to smelt iron and worked it—or wrought it—to produce weapons with a durable and lasting edge. Swords and spears were made in more varieties and improved in quality. As the secret of making wrought iron became widely known, iron knives, scissors, axes, and plows as well as weapons came within the reach of everyone.

5 *Dagger and Spear*

Probably the most common personal weapon is the dagger. Short, sharp, deadly! Early Iron Age men used it, and it is still in use today. Very much like the knife, it is found in almost all cultures. Examples are the Gurkha *kukri* of Nepal, the Malayan *kris,* the Japanese *tanto,* and the Bornese *karong.* Other words used for essentially the same weapon are the poniard, the dirk, and the stiletto.

The spear too is one of the earliest and simplest weapons. The primitive weapon was made of a wooden shaft tipped with a sharp point. It was usually eight or nine feet long, though ancient Macedonian soldiers had spears twenty-one to twenty-four feet long. The point was first made of flint, then of bronze, and later of steel.

The medieval lance and pike evolved from the ancient spear. The pike has a long wooden shaft with a steel point, sometimes with a hook on the side, varying somewhat in length. In remote regions of the world primitive peoples still hunt and fight with spears, sometimes putting poison on the tips.

Dagger (Mycenae, 1600 B.C.)

6 *The Sword*

The sword—what a unique place it holds in the imagination! It symbolizes justice, peace, the state—even magic. In both legend and history, famous warriors have possessed swords with extraordinary powers.

Although a vast variety of swords can be found in cultures throughout the world, basically it is a simple weapon: a sharp blade ending in a hilt, cross guard, and pommel. It is related to the bronze dagger, only longer and stronger. The Iron Age developed the forged blade, as heated iron was hammered into the shape desired. In general, Europeans preferred the straight sword while people on other continents favored the curved one.

Persian sabre

By medieval times the sword had become highly symbolic. The sword was made holy by the church, and the cross shape it formed became both a protection against sin and a reminder that its owner must use it to defend the church against its enemies. The long, straight sword is often seen clasped in the hands of the carved effigies of knights lying atop their tombs.

Some swords were massive weapons, with blades thirty-five or more inches long. These "swords of war" were used by knights on horseback to deal enormous, sweeping, slashing blows.

During the Middle Ages noblemen, officers of state, and members of important guilds had special swords of even greater length carried in front of them wherever they went. It was a sign of their high status.

1 Samurai Style

In feudal Japan, knights called samurai were the sword-bearing class. Japanese swordplay became an art as well as a skill, with carefully observed rules that typified the Japanese concern for style in all aspects of life.

Samurai helmet

"Style," says the military historian John Keegan, "was central to the samurai way of life—style in clothing, armor, weapons, skill-at-arms and behavior on the battlefield." (Not very different from their contemporaries, the knights of France and England.) In the Japanese manual of arms the sword was the central weapon.

Samurai swords, with family names inscribed on them, were often handed down from father to son, generation after generation. Samurai swords of top quality are the best-edged weapons ever made. One authority records that Japanese swordsmiths "hammered and folded and re-hammered, day after day, until a sword blade contained something like four million layers of finely forged steel."

But by the sixteenth century this Japanese sword-bearing class faced the challenge of firearms. The samurai realized that to allow these deadly new weapons to reach the hands of peasant soldiers would end the domination of sword-wielding warriors that had endured for a thousand years. Rather than adapting to a new type of warfare, the samurai barred weapons that used gunpowder, and closed off their island nation to contact with the outside world—a ban that lasted for 300 years, until new leadership chose to enter the age of weapons made by modern industry.

8 *Bayonets*

Over the centuries the design of swords gradually moved toward lighter and thinner weapons. By 1500 the old, bulky, rigid blade of the armored knight was giving way to the rapier—a straight, two-edged sword with a narrow, pointed blade, used chiefly for thrusting. Then, in the seventeenth century, the bayonet was invented, and sword and gun were combined into a single weapon.

Early versions of the bayonet were short steel daggers that fitted onto the muzzle of a musket. Of course, a soldier using that kind of bayonet couldn't fire his gun. A ring bayonet was soon introduced, and then a tubular socket that permitted the soldier to slip his bayonet around the barrel of his gun, so that he could continue to fire it. The bayonet replaced the pike. It made the musketeer his own pikesman.

9 *Cleaving the Skull*

Axlike weapons with heads of flint attached to a wooden handle were used in the Stone Age. Later, axheads of bronze and then of iron or steel were developed. The ax handles changed too. They became longer and longer. Axes five feet or longer were called poleaxes.

In the Battle of Hastings in 1066, the Saxons defending England at first did well using their great two-handed double-bladed poleaxes against the Norman troops of William the Conqueror. But the Norman invaders, with their fast-moving cavalry and archers armed with cross-bows, finally prevailed. The weapons in that battle are depicted in the Bayeux Tapestry, a beautiful weaving that

War hammer

tells the story of the Norman conquest of England.

Axlike weapons took different forms outside Europe. The American Indians used the tomahawk as a hatchet or throwing ax. In India, Japan, and the South Sea islands, elaborate decorative touches were added to war axes. But no matter how artistic the craftsmen, the object of the ax was the same: to cleave the skull of the enemy.

10 *David and Goliath*

One of the most ancient weapons is the sling. It was by the sling that young David (c. 1010–970 B.C.) slew the Philistine giant Goliath. You remember that story in the Old Testament of the Bible?

The men of Israel were in the valley of Elah, ready to fight with the Philistines. When the soldiers saw the enemy's champion, the towering figure of Goliath, they were frightened and ran away. All except little David, the youngest of eight brothers.

When Goliath saw a mere boy approaching him on the battlefield, he said disdainfully, Come ahead, and I will carve you up to feed the birds of the air and the beasts of the field! To which David replied, You have a sword and a spear and a shield, but I have the God of the armies of Israel.

David ran toward Goliath and, putting a stone in his sling, hurled it at the giant, striking him on the forehead and knocking him out. Then he snatched up Goliath's sword and cut off his head, and when the Philistines saw their champion was dead, they fled. It was this same David who later became a famous king of Israel.

The sling was the first missile launcher. Missiles are weapons that can be thrown from the hand, or from an instrument or engine, with the intent of striking an object at a distance.

Early man made slings out of two long strips of pliable hide, sinew, leather, or chord. One end of each of the two strips was attached to the sides of the pouch, which would hold the stone. David released his missile by twirling the sling around and around his head to gain momentum and then letting go of one strip at the right moment. An expert slinger can hurl his missile up to 500 yards.

The armies of the ancient world—Egypt, Greece, Rome, Persia—included companies of slingers. In Europe the weapon's use continued until the 1500s.

Slings are still used by people around the world—and to great effect.

Another propulsion device called the atlatl was used extensively by the Indians of North and South America. They attached a spear to a throwing-stick, which was whipped overhead to propel the spear through the air. This weapon was used up to about A.D. 1200, when it was replaced by the bow and arrow.

11 *With a Puff of Air*

Another weapon almost as old as the sling is the blowpipe, sometimes called the blowgun. It is simply a long, hollow tube with a small feathered dart inserted at one end. The warrior places the other end in his mouth, and with a puff of air from his lungs, the missile is shot out.

The dart's power to injure is greatly increased by dipping it in an active poison, such as curare. A poisoned dart may not pierce the victim's skin deeply—but its effect is almost immediate.

The people of equatorial Africa and the Indians of South America prized the blowpipe and used it effectively in warfare.

12 *The Shield*

When prehistoric man saw an enemy approaching—perhaps armed with a sling or spear or bow and arrow—his instinctive reaction was to take cover. The nearest tree or boulder would do. But in time he learned to devise a more active means of defense. A shield, held almost always in the left hand or worn on the left arm, offered protection and left the right arm free to wield a weapon.

The earliest shields were made of wood or wickerwork covered with animal hides. By 1000 B.C. shields were being made of bronze. These were usually two feet in diameter and circular in form. A grip handle was riveted onto the back.

Later craftsmen created other variations. Egyptians and Ethiopians made large rectangular shields that would protect a soldier from his neck to the ground. German warriors often painted their big round shields in brilliant colors. The Norman cavalrymen used kite-shaped shields, holding the broad upper part close to their eyes with their left hands, so as to protect the greater part of their bodies, while the tapering lower end covered their left thighs.

Strangely, most European soldiers at first refused any kind of protective covering except for the shield. To use more was thought to be unmanly, undignified. Asian soldiers, however, didn't object to greater safety. Thus it was in the East that body armor originated, and in time spread to Europe.

Roman shield

13 *Armor*

Armor is anything that is worn on the body to protect it. Nowadays when we think of armor, we think of the big metal suits knights wore. But earlier, before the Bronze Age, lighter and less expensive materials were used—skins, quilted cloth, hardened leather.

The Assyrians, whose empire reached its peak in the eighth century B.C., devised a scale armor. It was made of very small metal plates sewn on a leather jacket so that the rows overlapped. It gave Assyrian warriors great mobility in battle. Around A.D. 1100 chain-mail armor became popular in Europe. It covered the torso and even included a hood worn under a close-fitting helmet. A century later sleeves were lengthened and mittens and leg coverings were added. Later, the joints were reinforced with armor plate. By 1400 complete plate armor had come into fashion in Europe.

Around this time infantry became important enough in combat to wear armor. Most soldiers had headpieces of some kind to protect the body and, since they could afford nothing like the noblemen's costly armor, made use of any material they could find. Breastplates and shirts of mail were common. Some soldiers wore leather or cloth jackets closely studded with metal scales. If a soldier could do no better, he wore a quilted jerkin (sleeveless jacket).

The evolution of warfare, with the need to move rapidly more and more typically part of battle strategy, reduced the importance of personal armor. This happened even before firearms hastened the disappearance of armor in combat. By 1600 the role of knights had shrunk to almost nothing as infantry took the brunt of battle.

After 1600, when gunpowder was increasingly in use, Renaissance

craftsmen designed armor more for aesthetic appeal than for utility. This armor was often very costly; it was a mark of the high rank of the wearer. The aristocracy showed off their fashionable armor while jousting in competitive tournaments rather than using it in war.

14 *Taming the Horse*

The taming of the horse changed the nature of war. It happened long after people had domesticated cattle, sheep, goats, dogs, and pigs. Archeologists have found evidence that people living about 3500 B.C. in a small settlement in what is now Ukraine, a part of the vast Asian-European territory, kept herds of horses. These were wild animals rounded up for meat when needed, or for hides or the milk from mares. The pastoral people of this region were probably the first to tame and ride horses.

Gradually they learned to use the horses' power by harnessing them for pulling loads. With the invention of the wheel, a load could be placed in a cart or wagon, which in turn was improved over the centuries. When the light, spoked wheel was developed, it led to the invention of the chariot.

Now a revolutionary change in warfare was possible. A horse-drawn wheeled vehicle that could serve as a mobile platform for archers made warrior societies mobile and predatory.

In the ancient world the horse was used primarily for fighting with chariots. Mounted cavalry was never the primary fighting force in that era.

15 *Battle Chariots*

Chariots were first used in war about 2500 B.C. In the armies of ancient Egypt, Assyria, Greece, and Persia the elite striking force was usually made up of chariots. Nobleman and kings rode to battle in them.

The early chariots were heavy, clumsy, and slow moving. Lighter models replaced them, providing greater speed and mobility.

Most chariots were two-wheeled wooden platforms that rode about 16 inches off the ground. The back of the chariot was open, but a wraparound shield on the front and sides partially protected the crew. Two horses, one on each side of a pole attached to the front, pulled the chariot. Sometimes three and even four animals were attached to the traces for greater speed.

The crew? Two men, an archer or spearman and the driver, with the former always in command. Sometimes sharp blades or scythes were fastened to the ends of the axles so that when chariots were driven through enemy ranks their soldiers were sliced up. One Assyrian king described the havoc caused by his charioteers when they fought the Elamites in 691 B.C.: "My prancing steeds, trained to harness, plunged into their welling blood as into a river; the wheels of my battle chariots were bespattered with blood and filth. I filled the plains with the corpses of their warriors."

Chariot (Monteleone, sixth century B.C.)

16 *From Primitive to Modern*

Making war, often with no particular goal, was part of many early cultures. Sometimes war was an activity that held more of a ritualistic than rational meaning. Anthropologists have found warfare present in most of the cultures they have studied. War in these societies often meant brief, limited action, action that tested the warriors' skills and gained them glory, yet left them—and their enemies—pretty much unharmed.

An American anthropologist, Harry Turney-High, who served in the U.S. cavalry, has described in detail the nature of combat in many different cultures. He has told how people in Vanuatu (an island group in the South Pacific) appoint champions to stage ritual duels before the assembled opposing sides. In North America, among the Assinboin, the men who dreamed of victory over an enemy were accepted as war leaders. The Iroquois supported tribal police to make sure no one would run away from battle.

The practice of "primitive" war changes, Turney-High asserted, when a state comes into existence that employs an army with officers to conduct its wars. That is the distinction now accepted between "primitive" war and "civilized" or "modern" war.

Many anthropologists have made field studies of warfare among primitive societies. If you look into the descriptions of warfare in some groups, such as the Maoris of New Zealand, the Maring of New Guinea, the Aztecs of Mexico, or hundreds of others we could list, you find great differences in the practice of warfare. It is hard to generalize about the nature of such warfare. There are exceptions to almost any rule one might try to establish. Many researchers have concluded that there is an inborn urge in all cultures to be aggressive. It is expressed in two ways: the impulse of the individual to guard one's own particular territory, and that of the tribe to secure its survival.

Killing as a means of exercising or gaining power entered man's consciousness during many different periods of time. And warfare—the art of mass attack and defense—became the terrible ever-present danger in human affairs.

The ritual or primitive nature of warfare changed in at least one part of the world when out of the Eurasian heartland came invaders on horseback and in chariots who imposed their power on dwellers in the settled lands to the west. Charioteers easily overran foot soldiers, taking prisoners and enslaving them. Dreading invasion, the peoples of Europe had to organize their own societies on a military basis. Out of that need rose methods of fighting in a disciplined way. Both infantry and cavalry tried to fight decisive battles, battles that would not just drive out the enemy but crush it once and for all. However, in order to achieve that goal, one had to be willing to accept heavy losses of one's own people.

17 *The Horse People*

The taming of the horse made fighting from chariots possible. It also led to the creation of another military force, the cavalry. Mounted troops trained to fight from horseback appeared first on the steppe around 1000 B.C. The steppe is a huge belt of grassland, 3,000 miles long and averaging 500 miles in depth. On the north it is bounded by the subarctic and on the south by deserts and mountains. On the eastern end it reaches into China and on the western the approaches to the fertile lands of the Middle East and Europe. A treeless, grassy plain between the mountains, it isn't suitable for agriculture unless heavily irrigated, but its grazing grounds are suitable for raising horses, cattle, and sheep.

The Scythians were among the earliest people of the steppe to fight on horseback. They flourished from the eighth to the fourth centuries B.C. They invaded Assyria, a military power to the south that also fielded cavalry on a large scale. The Scythians had to enlist the aid of allies to break the power of Assyria.

The Persians relied on the chariot rather than on cavalry, but they lost their empire when the mounted troops of young Alexander the Great overcame them in the great Battle of Issus in 333 B.C. Persian losses were about 50,000 killed, while Alexander lost about 450 men.

The Huns too were a steppe people who conducted warfare from horseback. Their cavalry invaded the Roman Empire in the fifth century A.D. The Huns derived enormous wealth in gold by demanding ransom for military and civilian captives, as well as by requiring bribes from emperors anxious to stave off attack. Commanded at their peak by Attila, the Huns disappeared from history after the death of Attila and his sons.

But other military powers would continue to rely on the horse for conquest. Cavalries would threaten Europe, the Middle East, and Asia for a thousand years.

18 *The Cavalry: Rise and Fall*

When Charlemagne (742?–814), came to the throne of the Franks in 771, it marked the beginning of a new era in the European art of war from horseback. He waged war on a vast scale by greatly increasing the number of mounted men in his armies. Europe's rulers up to then had used only small groups of mounted bodyguards, cavalry drawn from the aristocrats.

Charlemagne made military service compulsory in every region he conquered. He required lords and bishops, and all who held tenants on royal or church lands, to enter his army "with horse and arms, shield, lance, sword, and dagger." Anyone who failed that obligation was heavily fined, and might forfeit life and property. The practice continued throughout the feudal period.

Making conquest after conquest, Charlemagne gained control over most of Europe. In 800, the Pope at Rome crowned him Emperor of the West.

Later it was cavalry warfare that marked the Crusades—that series of wars between the eleventh and fourteenth centuries, during which Christian Europeans fought unsuccessfully to recover the Holy Land from the Muslims. The incredible military victories of the Mongols in the thirteenth century were also based on the power of cavalry. Napoleon too made great use of mounted troops in his many wars, and later so did both sides in the American Civil War.

But with the development of the machine gun and trench warfare in World War I, the value of cavalry diminished. By World War II, the new mobile tank units made cavalry almost completely obsolete.

19 *Defend Yourself!*

If somebody hits you, your immediate reaction is to defend yourself. So it is with communities, nations, empires—people seek ways to defend their lives and their homes. So it was even in Jericho, the oldest known settlement in the world, dating back to about 8000 B.C.

Archeologists excavating this town of ancient Palestine found it had been fortified by walls and a tower. Fortifications were not only a refuge for short-term safety but a stronghold for active defense. Such centers made defenders secure from surprise; they were also a base from which soldiers could move out against attackers.

Almost all strongholds throughout the Middle East, Asia, Africa, and Europe had three defensive features: walls, moat, and tower. Little more was added to them in the 9,000 years between the construction of Jericho and the introduction of gunpowder in the thirteenth century.

Strongholds sprang up in regions where no central authority had been established. When a great state such as the Persian Empire held sway, its center was defended at its outer limits. During the rise of the Roman Empire the cities within it were undefended. Fortifications were built only along the frontiers.

But after the decline of Roman power, when its frontiers were overrun by barbarian invaders, most of western Europe was left with few internal fortifications. After the Dark Ages, as feudalism developed, warlords ruled small principalities and kingdoms. With trade and town life reviving, funds became available to build defenses against dangers from beyond the walls.

Local strongmen soon covered the face of Europe with castles. The function of castles was both to provide a refuge and to dominate an area.

At first simply built, castles became larger and more powerful stone strongholds. Local barons lived inside them, stabled their warhorses there, and housed their men-at-arms. As local lords struggled for domination over one another, warfare spread like disease.

The methods of siege and the engines used did not originate in the Middle Ages. They go way back to Jericho and the ancient world. In the Middle East, North Africa, and elsewhere archeologists have unearthed battering rams and movable towers, the basic siege weapons, as well as scaling ladders and mineshafts. The Greeks also used catapults to hurl projectiles over walls.

Around 8000 B.C. engineers were digging mineshafts to penetrate beneath walls, and building mobile towers to reach the crests of walls. They devised huge shields made of wicker or wood to protect operators of siege engines who were within range of weapons on the walls. Whenever possible, attackers cut off the water supply and starved out defenders.

But besiegers too had their problems. Weather might go bad, men might desert, food might give out before the castle's supply did. Even if the besieger broke through the walls, he might find himself in a trap or, once inside, have to fight his way up steep, winding stairways under constant attack from the defenders.

These methods of attack and defense continued for thousands of years, down into feudal times. The advantage in siege warfare, before gunpowder, was all on the side of defense. So widely accepted was this fact that in western Europe the two opposing sides sometimes agreed on a time limit. If the siege had not been successful by the set date, a truce began and the people within the walls could march out in safety.

20 *The Unsung Diggers and Builders*

To achieve security against attack, military leaders and their engineers gave orders for excavation or construction that caused untold numbers of people great suffering.

In the time of imperial Rome, Julius Caesar had no rival in the art of siege war. Much of what he accomplished had less to do with science or engineering than with the immense labor of digging. In a siege of 52 B.C., the Romans shifted 2.6 million cubic yards of earth from trenches. In another siege, they dug a trench fifteen feet deep, fifteen feet broad, and thirty-four miles long.

Hadrian's Wall, seventy-three miles long, stretches across the narrow part of the island of Britain. It was built between A.D. 122 and 126, when the Roman emperor Hadrian decided to close the frontier against wild tribes living in the north. His defense works included the stone wall, six feet high and eight feet thick, plus mile stations of blockhouses and turrets.

But that line of defense seems a minor effort compared with the Great Wall of China, completed much earlier, in 211 B.C. This gigantic undertaking, winding 1,500 miles across northern China, was erected to protect China from nomads to the north. Laborers were conscripted from all over the country to build it, at the cost of terrible suffering and many deaths. The wall, made of stone blocks and earth, averages twenty-five feet high and fifteen to thirty feet thick at the base, sloping to twelve feet at the top. Guard stations and watchtowers were built at regular intervals. But invaders from the north penetrated the wall often, proving this massive defense was not of great value.

An even more incredible military feat was the bridging of the Dardanelles—also called the Hellespont—in ancient times. The Dardanelles are a forty-mile-long strait that connects the Mediterranean with the Black Sea. In 481 B.C. an engineer designed two floating roadways, made of fifty-oared galleys that were covered over. The galleys were linked by six cables, two of flax and four of papyrus. The pontoon bridge at the western end had 314 galleys; that at the eastern end had 360. The vast bridges made possible the invasion of Greece by its Persian enemy, Xerxes. No military engineers attempted anything of this magnitude again until modern times.

21 *You Did What You Could*

What could people in a castle or fortified town do to defend themselves when under attack? We've seen the methods and machines of the besieger. But those under siege had no special equipment for defense. They could pour boiling oil or molten lead from their walls down upon the heads of the assault troops. They could lob incendiary material onto the enemy camp, pour liquid fire over the battering rams and movable towers, shoot arrows through the slits in their walls, or hurl stones and bolts from ballistas—huge crossbows—mounted on the ramparts.

There were no fixed rules for defense. You did what you could. As one military expert wrote, "Stout hearts, determination and enterprise in the face of pestilence, starvation, fire and death were the only reliable qualities to sustain a beleaguered garrison. Surrender was out of the question since it spelt slavery or extermination for the men and concubinage for the women. . . ."

But surrender some did. The story of the siege of Famagusta, a fortress on the island of Cyprus, is a terrible one. Cyprus was an outpost of the Venetians, defended by them against the Turks, who were seeking to extend the power of Islam deep into Europe. The ships of Selim, the

Cannon

Turkish leader, had brought 250,000 men up to the walls of Famagusta. His huge cannons, specifically built for the task, made great breaches in the Venetian fortifications. The gunners fired 150,000 balls during the siege, which began in the spring of 1571. For months the city held out, causing the Turks over 50,000 casualties. But finally the situation of the Venetian garrison and the townspeople became intolerable. On August 1 the Venetian commander, Marcantonio Bragadino, was forced to accept Selim's terms of surrender.

Enraged by Famagusta's resistance and the price it had cost his men, Selim decided to make an example of Bragadino by punishing him in the cruelest way. He held a public mock execution, cut off Bragadino's nose and ears, and forced him to crawl around the city, kissing the ground. Then he had the commander flayed alive, stuffed the corpse with straw, paraded it through the streets, and symbolically placed it in a slave prison.

The horrifying fall of Famagusta strengthened the growing resistance to the Turkish invaders.

22 *The Main Purpose Changes*

Warfare dominated the world of Europe from the ninth to the seventeenth centuries. In that long passage of time many features of war changed: the causes for which people fought, the weapons, the tactics, and the relations between leaders and followers.

The patterns followed by Germanic and Celtic warfare were typical of the earlier centuries. Farmers fought one season and tilled their land the next. They went to war for loot, for land, or for honor. The epic poems and songs of that era tell of men fighting hand to hand, with axes and heavy swords, turning streams red with blood and fields white with rotting corpses.

By the eleventh century the obligation to fight had changed from an occasional fixed duty owed a chieftain to the main purpose in the warrior's life.

23 *Knife and Staff*

Useful tools of everyday living may be turned into deadly weapons.

Back in medieval England everyone, including women, carried a knife. If you sat down somcwhcrc to cat, you were expected to bring your own knife.

Almost as common was the quarterstaff, the heavy wooden stick carried both for herding animals and for helping you walk on the muddy roads.

Both knife and quarterstaff did serious damage when quarrels broke out among farmers in the fields. They were struggling to survive, and took insults to their honor very seriously. Violence was the accepted method of settling disputes, for who had the patience to wait for justice in the king's slow-moving courts? So out came the knife to stab, or the quarterstaff to bludgeon, with deadly results.

24 *Hitting the Head*

There is a class of personal weapons called *concussive*. Hit on the head with such a weapon, the victim is stunned or killed. Wooden clubs and stone hammers were the first concussive weapons.

When metals were discovered, iron spikes were added to increase the club's power to do damage. Called a mace, this heavy weapon was used in the Middle Ages to smash a knight's armor. A simple mace could be made by driving nails into a club, and the cheap weapon became popular among the peasants of Europe.

Another adaptation was called the military flail. It was a shaft to which were attached several whips made of chain, each ending with a studded ball. Swung by an expert, the flail could inflict serious injury.

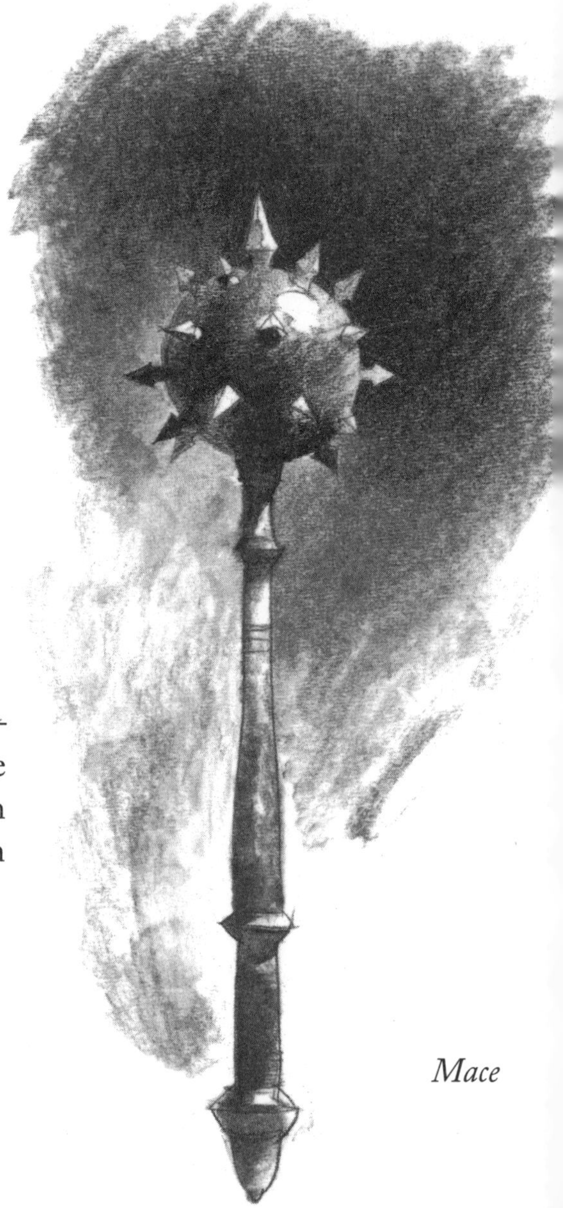

Mace

25 *The Hundred Years War*

Have you heard of the Hundred Years War?

Did that mean people went on killing each other for a whole century?

Who was crazy enough to do that?

England and France, that's who. Or rather, not the English people or the French, but their rulers, greedy for more power and wealth and indifferent to the cost in terms of their citizens' lives.

The cause was a quarrel over which country controlled what land. The roots of the quarrel can be traced back to when William of Normandy crossed over from France and conquered England in 1066. He then ruled over a state that lay on both sides of the English Channel.

The Hundred Years War itself broke out in 1337, when an English king declared himself to be the king of France as well, a title already possessed by a French king. That did it. The war was really a series of eight major conflicts between the royal houses of England and France. Battles were waged, and power and possessions tilted first to one side, then to the other, for well over a hundred years. At the end, in 1453, the only piece of France with which England was left was the French port of Calais (which France was to win back a hundred years later).

What was the net gain—or loss—of that interminable war? For France, it brought mass misery. Its farmlands were devastated and its population was savagely reduced by war, by famine, and by the Black Plague. Roving bands of armed killers looted and terrorized the countryside. Civil wars and local wars broke out, increasing the destruction. Society fell apart. The feudal nobility of France was ruined, which led to much greater power concentrated in the hands of the king.

As for England, while it lost its holdings on the continent, as well as great numbers of soldiers, it began to expand as a sea power elsewhere around the world.

From a military point of view, that interminable war saw the return of infantry soldiers to predominance on the battlefield. In the Battle of Crécy (1346) the English combined the defensive capability of heavily armed pikemen with the speed and firepower of light archers using the crossbow, while cavalry was employed for counterattack. The English won a stunning victory over a French force nearly three times its size, boasting the finest cavalry in Europe. The use of gunpowder weapons in battle in Europe had begun decades earlier, but in the Hundred Years War both the English and French introduced crude cannons on the battlefield and in siege warfare.

26 *Warriors Come First*

Most societies teach skills with weapons only to their male children. Very few cultures are known in which women are specifically trained to be as warlike or as aggressive as men. It is the males who are pushed to be aggressive, and the females are trained to be submissive and obedient to them.

Where males have sole control over weapons and the training to use them, it is easy to see how men can come to dominate women—either by threatening force or by actually using it.

Many cultures, research has shown, move from taking part in war to male dominance, to the creation of a warrior culture. Fighting in combat becomes the most important thing a man can do. The men risk their lives for family and the community, which makes them highly esteemed. And women therefore are valued less than men. They must depend on the protection of the warriors.

Evidence of the high place accorded warriors in Europe's prehistoric societies has been found by archeologists. In Mycenae, an ancient city of Greece founded about 2000 B.C., most of the objects unearthed were either weapons or household objects that portrayed warriors. Once such a warrior culture developed, its values were passed on to future generations. The values came to be seen as both natural and inevitable. Beliefs, stories, and religions justified and glorified war and male warriors.

You find this when you read the earliest writings of these cultures. Remember the Greek epics of Homer. Or take the laws of ancient Rome, called the Twelve Tables. Or the first five books of the Old Testament, called the Pentateuch. The ancient Greeks, Romans, Hebrews—all cherished the courage and daring of the warrior.

27 *Do Women War?*

Fighting wars is the one activity from which women, with minor exceptions, have always and everywhere been excluded, not necessarily by choice; rather, this was a male-enforced pattern. However, it is true that women have sometimes been the cause of war, or at least peripherally involved in war. The fabled Helen—regarded in Greek myth as the most beautiful woman in the world—was said to have triggered the Trojan War. According to the Greek poet Homer, the war was caused when Paris, the son of King Priam of Troy, fell in love with Helen, the wife of King Menelaus of Sparta, and carried her off to Troy. The Greek leaders then joined in an expedition to war against Troy.

When a war is brewing, women have sometimes challenged their menfolk to rally to the flag, implying cowardice if some are reluctant to make the heroic sacrifice. But only rarely have women themselves fought. Not until the last few decades of the twentieth century has the U.S. government permitted women to serve in anything other than support roles and enter combat units. Nonetheless, while warfare is universal, it has been almost entirely a male activity.

28 *The Amazons: Women Warriors?*

But weren't there women warriors too? Early on? What about the Amazons?

No one has yet found sure proof of a female society of Amazon warriors. However, Greek culture portrays them repeatedly. The frieze of sculptures atop the Parthenon of Athens contains the figures of Amazons. These women warriors were supposed to have besieged Athens around 1200 B.C. Amazons are mentioned twice in Homer's *Iliad*, and they appear in several Greek legends. Theseus married an Amazon, and Achilles fell in love with their queen, Penthesilea, as she lay dying from a blow he struck. And then there is Hercules: One of his labors was to steal the girdle of an Amazon queen.

The Greek historian Herodotus, writing in the fifth century B.C., said he believed the Amazons came from Asia. And women's tombs excavated east of the Don River in Eurasia were found to contain swords, spears, arrows, and even a full set of armor. So whether or not there was an all-female Amazon society, certainly some women were warriors in early society.

29 *Heroic Women*

Women in the Old Testament of the Hebrews are sometimes shown in the heroic roles usually played by men. Jael killed an enemy general by hammering a nail into his head. And

Judith slew the enemy general Holofernes by slicing off his head with his own sword. Then, displaying the severed head to the Hebrew troops, she rallied them on to victory.

Epics of the Germans and Celts also portray women warriors. There are the Valkyries of Norse legend: warrior maidens, usually represented as riding through the air on horseback, helmeted and carrying spears. Queen Maeve of the Celts ruled equally with her husband and fought independently of him. Warrior women of other nations led revolts against Roman power, according to the historian Tacitus.

Much later, in the feudal world of the ninth to twelfth centuries, some European women waged war just like men. Matilda, the daughter of Henry I of England, led her own armies against feudal lords who contested her right to the throne in the twelfth century. Isabella of Castile married Ferdinand of Aragon in 1469, uniting the two kingdoms to create the powerful empire of Spain. Both with Ferdinand and on her own, she warred with Portugal, put down revolts, and supervised the war to drive the Moors out of Granada, their last stronghold in Europe.

30 *The Military Life*

Military life is the most highly organized existence short of prison. Soldiers are *standardized.* Note the name for the clothing they are obliged to wear—*uniform.* Soldiers must not only rise on time, but sergeants stand by to make sure they do. They must not only obey superiors, but show their obligation to do so any time they meet officers by saluting them. It's understood they are saluting the officer's insignia of rank, not the person. The aim of such required behavior is to make soldiers act automatically if one officer falls in combat and another takes his place.

After all, a military leader's battle plans are worth little if subordinates do not predictably carry them out. So subordinates are not supposed to question orders, change them, or decide which are to be obeyed and which not. The soldier is a numbered unit in larger numbered units and promoted or demoted by set standards. The military is a bureaucratic life if ever there was one.

31 *New Goal in War*

In the time of Napoleon (1769–1821), the general who made himself emperor of France, the nature of European war changed radically. Before the French Revolution of 1789, armies of the old regime were held to be precious. The officer corps were noblemen, not to be recklessly wasted in war. They were professionals, trained at great expense to command costly mercenary troops. The army's prime aim was not only to protect the regime's territory, but also to protect itself. Kings fought kings in limited wars, usually for some narrow goal. Kings did not want to overthrow kingship itself.

But the French Revolution turned everything upside down. The new army of France was made up of ordinary people in arms. These masses were conscripted to provide resistance to the encircling powers of Europe, which threatened the people's revolution. Napoleon's military goal was to destroy attacking armies, no matter what the cost to his own troops. With the French nobility both the enemy of the revolution and its victim, Napoleon's officers were no longer aristocrats but talented men of the middle class. With plenty of officers to draw upon and huge numbers in the rank and file, Napoleon threw his armies into war with a new recklessness. He developed a new kind of warfare—to fight not for position or territory, but to completely destroy the opposing troops.

32 *Gunpowder and Guns*

Ultimately the engines invented for siege warfare could not resist the pressure of progress. The introduction of gunpowder in Europe in the thirteenth century signaled their passing. And as the power of artillery increased, all the devices developed to attack or defend castles and strongholds vanished from the battlefield.

Almost no one at that time in the Middle Ages had any idea of the vast changes the introduction of gunpowder would bring about. Yet its impact upon the peoples of the world and on warfare in particular would be profound. It changed the balance of power wherever it was used, and changed the scale of warfare as nothing else would until the release of atomic and thermonuclear energy at the close of World War II.

Where did gunpowder come from? The Chinese, around the tenth century A.D., discovered that a mixture of potassium nitrate (saltpeter), charcoal, and sulfur produced a compound that had explosive effects. The Chinese seem to have used it mostly as a noisemaker or for semimagical rites in temples around 950 A.D., but not in warfare, so far as we know, at least until the thirteenth century. This was about the same time that Europeans recognized the military usefulness of explosive power.

How the next step came about—placing gunpowder and a projectile in a tube and detonating the powder to produce a force that would shoot the projectile out—no one knows. But

Leonardo da Vinci's war invention

art gives us a clue to the approximate date. A drawing in an English illuminated manuscript of 1326 shows a gun shaped like a vase, with a large shaft or arrow sticking out of its neck, mounted on four legs, and a gunner applying a priming iron or igniter to the touchhole to fire the shaft at a castle gate opposite. This was a gun, however strange it may look to us. A gun, in essence, is a metal tube from which a missile or projectile is shot by the force of exploding gunpowder or some other propellant.

Progress in this new form of weaponry was slow. Not until the fifteenth century did cannonballs replace arrows and the gun take on a more tubular form. Such cannons were used in siege warfare to break down walls, but they were not very effective on the battlefield. They were too big, too heavy, and not mobile. In the early 1490s French craftsmen developed cannons light enough to be transported on wheels so that they could be moved at the same speed as the army. The new cannon was a slender bronze tube, about eight feet long, that fired wrought-iron balls and was easily maneuvered on a small cart drawn by horses. It could be moved swiftly into action close to a wall, and then fired accurately in a predictable arc to smash through the stonework.

While artillery experts improved their weapon, fortress engineers developed new designs to lessen the destructive power of cannons. Big money was paid for the work, and even great artist-inventors like Leonardo da Vinci and Michelangelo studied the problem and created new defenses.

All through Europe, the Middle East, and West Africa an international class of technical experts sold their skills to rulers eager to acquire better cannons and better defenses against them. By 1600 the frontiers of every state had placed modern bastion fortresses wherever attempts to attack could be expected.

33 *The Devil's Invention*

Gunpowder, it might be noted, was considered the devil's invention in the England of Shakespeare's time. One of the most famous episodes in that country's history is the Gunpowder Plot. It was a conspiracy to blow up the English Parliament and King James I on November 5, 1605, the day set for the king to open Parliament. Had it succeeded, it would have destroyed the entire British government.

It was meant to be the signal for a great uprising of English Catholics, who were being savagely persecuted for their religious beliefs by the Protestant regime. The plotters had secretly hidden thirty-six barrels of gunpowder in a cellar under the House of Lords. But the plot was exposed almost at the last minute and the conspirators were executed. One of them was Guy Fawkes, a soldier expert in the use of gunpowder. The date set for the explosion is celebrated with fireworks and bonfires in England every November 5, Guy Fawkes Day.

34 *Only One of Twenty*

The flintlock gun, invented in France, was widely used in Europe by 1650. Soon thereafter, both European settlers in the Americas and the Native Americans took enthusiastically to the weapon. Once adopted, it held sway for about 200 years.

Weighing ten pounds, the flintlock was not a handy gun. It took forty seconds for a well-trained soldier to load and fire a single shot. Its accuracy? Terrible. Only at short range was it effective. A soldier could hit a foot-square target nearly every time—but at a distance of only forty yards.

Guy Fawkes

Place a target eighteen square feet at 300 yards, and only one out of twenty bullets would hit it.

With a gun like the flintlock there was little value in training troops for marksmanship. Training was mostly for toughening legs for marching and the body for combat. So from the mid-1600s to the late 1700s, officers had their men advance in battle shoulder to shoulder, perhaps two or three lines deep, at eighty steps per minute. Since the flintlock was no good for long-range combat, soldiers were trained to hold fire till the last minute. Then the side that fired first had to reload—remember forty seconds?—while the enemy ran and fired their bullets in at an even closer range.

The carnage was appalling. Only rigid discipline kept troops reloading, advancing, and firing while all around them men's blood and guts poured into the earth.

35 *Strange Weapons*

Imagine the impact of a gun upon a people who had never seen or heard of such a weapon. When Hernán Cortés, the Spanish conquistador, marched into central Mexico in 1519, he found a people who had created a highly organized civilization. To the Spanish, however, the Aztecs were barbarians to be conquered, converted to Christianity, and looted of everything valuable.

Cortés had about 300 men, among them 40 armed with crossbows and 20 with matchlock guns, a type of gun developed only very recently in Europe. Made of wrought iron, the matchlock guns were about four feet long and able to fire metal balls or stones of two or three pounds. The Spanish also had three pieces of artillery, which they carried on carts. These were the first wheeled vehicles in the Americas, and were no doubt nearly as astonishing to the Indians as those strange animals, the horses,

that pulled the artillery carts. The Aztecs' weapons were wooden swords with obsidian-edged blades, bows and arrows, lances, and slings.

The Indians could shoot their arrows faster than the Spanish their guns. But the guns' "fiery lightning" and explosive noise, and the power of the projectiles, were terrifying to the native warriors. The gun proved decisive in the conquest of the Americas. The Indians managed to get guns later, chiefly by barter. But the Europeans had a great advantage: They controlled the source of the weapon—the gun factories.

36 *The Handgun: Miniature Cannon*

The first true handgun—the pistol—was developed around 1550. It seems to have been invented by a German, Johannes Kiefuss. His mechanism operated much like a modern cigarette lighter. A rough wheel rotated against a piece of iron pyrite to generate a spark. That ignited the powder in the weapon's flash pan. The wheel rotated when the trigger was pulled to release a heavy spring.

Cavalrymen often carried three pistols in combat in order to fire repeatedly at the enemy. They held two in holsters and a third in their right boot. After shooting all three pistols, they had to either reholster the last pistol and draw their sword or else ride off to reload the weapons, for that required both hands.

The pistol came into common use on the western frontier of America. The ordinary citizen had a gun in his pocket, and gamblers always toted a "shooting iron," for their profession was a dangerous one. These were usually derringers, small pistols with about an inch of barrel, easily hidden in a pocket. They fired a bullet half an inch in diameter and were effective only at limited range, but enough to get a man across the card table.

Wheel-lock pistol

The military had single-shot pistols, but some soldiers had double-barreled weapons and even pistols with four, five, or six barrels. In some guns the barrels had to be rotated by hand, but most operated by the pull of the trigger.

In 1836 the first widely used repeating pistol was invented by Samuel Colt of Hartford, Connecticut. Colt's weapon was a single-barreled pistol with five chambers bored into a revolving drum. Other types of revolvers had appeared before this time, but Colt was the first to make good, reliable ones by mass-production methods. Colts were used in the Mexican War and by the Texas Rangers against the Indians. Their firepower amazed the enemy.

Automatic pistols came along in the 1890s. These are really self-loading weapons; they don't fire themselves. A metal magazine containing bullets is slid into the butt of the gun, and the energy of the recoil is used to extract and load. To do this the barrel slides back a limited distance after firing. This gun was made in Germany. The first one to be made in America was the Colt .38, launched in 1900. It had an eight-shot magazine that slipped into the butt. The caliber was raised to .48 in 1905. (The higher the caliber, the larger the diameter of the bullet.) Soon after, the U.S. Army made the Colt the official sidearm.

As the production and quality of gunpowder were improved, firearms became more powerful. By the seventeenth century firearms and artillery had become the dominant weapons in warfare. Military leaders learned to fire guns in mass volleys, with devastating effect. Nonetheless, cavalries armed with swords and lances were still deployed in battle. Even as late as the Napoleonic wars at the beginning of the nineteenth century, and later in the American Civil War, such methods of pregun warfare survived.

37 *More Than a Tool*

Of all the tools the American pioneers carried into the wilderness, none was as important as the gun. It was the means of fending off predators, both animal and human, as well as killing game for food. But to many the gun was much more than a tool, and the care given to decorate it bordered on artistry.

Guns were often embellished with gold or ivory, or covered with fine engravings. They became the symbol of power, the emblem of rank, the reason for respect. The man with a gun felt he had the means to neutralize a hostile environment.

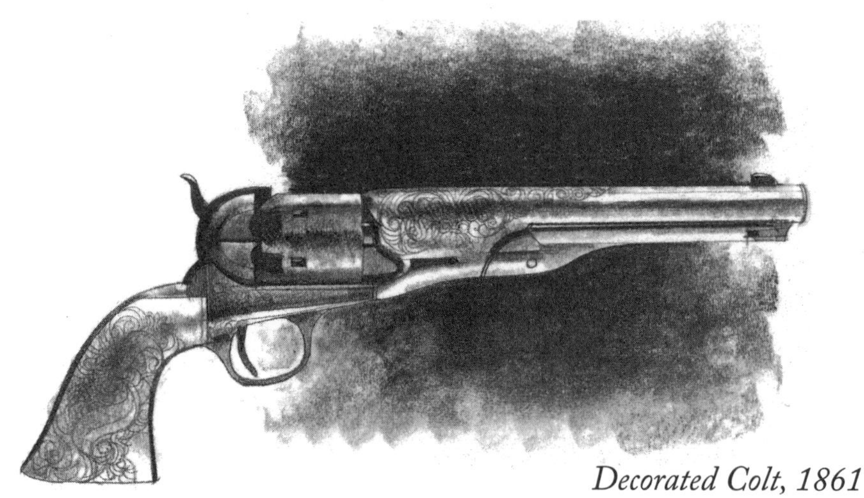

Decorated Colt, 1861

38 *Floating Platforms*

On land men may fight with fists, clubs, or guns. But how can they do that on the surface of the water? Only if they have a platform that will stay afloat. The origin of ships built especially for warfare is hard to trace, because wood decomposes easily. The earliest warship found dates back to about 6000 B.C.

It took wealth to build warships and to train the crews to handle them. Fighting on water cost more than fighting on land. But more than money was needed. You had to worry about suitable weather and a way to move your ships. Wind offers free power, and the earliest picture of naval warfare—a scene in Egypt from 1186 B.C.—shows a ship with sails. But sailing ships were not good platforms before the gun era. You couldn't easily get your ship close enough to the enemy's ships for hand-to-hand fighting with swords and spears. Ships propelled by oars were far better. But they had to be big enough to allow space for the food and water needed by large rowing crews. In bad weather oared ships are much harder to maneuver.

39 *Ships of the Viking Age*

The Vikings, who mastered ship construction and star-sight navigation, were able to make forays outside their own waters and to devastate lands great distances from their base. They depended on wind to move their longships to foreign shores and used oars chiefly for auxiliary power.

Helmet

Ships were the supreme achievement of the Vikings' technical skill and the foundation of their power. Three specimens of their vessels, excavated in Norway, tell us what their ships were like. (The ships can be seen today in the Viking Ship Museum just outside Oslo.) One of them, found in 1903, is especially well preserved. Built of oak, it is 71½ feet long, 17 feet wide, and nearly 5 feet deep from gunwale to keel. The 15 pairs of oars are 12 feet long, elegant and decorated. The prow too is decorated on each side with ornaments based on animal forms. The prow rises in a high spiral, ending in a snake's head.

The Viking sail slowly evolved from a small, not very useful square piece of cloth to a magnificent large sail, probably square, and colored either in blue-and-red stripes or solidly red.

The whole ship must have looked like a fabulous monster as it breasted the waves, its head and tail glistening, its stout body filled with men. The biggest Viking ships were probably twice as large as this one. All the Viking ships were designed for battle as well as commerce. Toward the end of the Viking era that unity of function ceased. Two separate types of ship were designed; one built for speed and mobility in battle, the other for its carrying capacity as a trading vessel.

The Viking longships were superior to the coast-hugging craft of other European powers. Their sailors were tough enough to bear the miseries of long voyages on uncovered hulls. The Vikings even carried horses aboard ship, so that the warriors could ride deep inland in search of loot and places to trade or settle. From Scandinavia their longships reached England, Germany, Spain, Iceland, Greenland, and North America long before Columbus sailed. They crossed the Baltic, too, and moved down the great Russian rivers to reach the land of Byzantium.

40 *The Battle of Lepanto*

One of the greatest naval battles in history was fought out in the waters of Greece. On October 7, 1571, in the narrow straits leading from the Gulf of Corinth, the forces of Islam and Christianity came together. Turkish sea power had been growing steadily. It threatened the dominant position of the Venetian fleet, which had previously monopolized control of the Mediterranean. To meet the great danger of Islamic sea power, Pope Pius V had cobbled together a Christian League with Venice and Spain. Their combined fleet assembled under the command of twenty-four-year-old Don John of Austria.

The Turkish admiral, Ali Pasha, had gathered ships for a campaign that would open all of Europe to his country's armies. This was still the age of galleys—vessels powered by oars. His first job was to secure a plentiful supply of slaves to man the oars of a great fleet. In the summer of 1571 he raided the coasts of Crete and other islands, kidnapping able young men in the villages. Their fate was to be chained for the rest of their lives to the oars of Turkish warships. By the time Ali's fleet neared Lepanto, 25,000 Greeks had been captured and placed at the oars of 200 galleys.

The Christian fleet had about the same number of ships. Don John decided to stake all on a massive naval battle. He knew that if he lost, nothing could prevent the Turks from advancing on the continent of Europe.

This would be the last great battle fought with oar-powered ships. Don John's flagship, *Real* (now on view in the Maritime Museum of Barcelona), fired the opening shot, and then the 400 ships began a furious close-quarters bombardment with cannons, harquebuses, longbows, and crossbows.

The Turks depended on boarding tactics, using their galleys simply as mobile platforms to enable foot soldiers to swarm onto the enemy's deck.

In contrast, the Christian fleet relied on cannon power. Don John had placed extra cannons on many of his galleys, making them highly mobile gun platforms. Spearheading his attack were six galleases—huge, clumsy vessels that had to be towed into action by smaller galleys. Each of these monsters carried forty heavy cannons, and their decks were packed with sharpshooters armed with guns firing balls that could pierce straight through a man at 200 yards.

The fleets, each stretched out over a five-mile crescent, met in a series of great clashes. Fighting raged for about three hours. Gradually the superior skill of the Christian sailors and the enormous firing power commanded by Don John caused appalling destruction of the foot soldiers crowding the Turkish decks and the naked galley slaves straining at their oars beneath.

The Turkish right flank was driven back against the shore and wiped out. Ali, on the left flank, managed to disengage and escape with 47 of his vessels. Turkish deaths totaled 30,000 out of 60,000 men engaged. Almost fifteen thousand Christian rowing slaves were freed from captured or sinking Turkish vessels, though at least 10,000 more must have gone down with their ships. The Christians lost 13 galleys, about 7,500 dead, and nearly 8,000 wounded. Among these was the young Miguel Cervantes, who lost the use of his left arm. Later he would write the classic novel *Don Quixote.*

"Lepanto," says the historian John Keegan, "was one of the world's decisive battles. This success of temporarily united Christendom ended the growing Turkish domination of the central and western Mediterranean, and marked the high tide of Islam's great threat against Christian Europe."

41 *The Spanish Armada*

Lepanto came near the end of the era of the war galley, which had lasted for nearly two thousand years. Galleys continued to operate in the Mediterranean for another hundred years. But such ships were merely auxiliaries to the broadside battery sailing ships. A new era began when admirals such as Sir John Hawkins realized the great power of naval gunfire.

Only seventeen years after Lepanto came the test: the sea battle between the Spanish Armada and the British fleet. Great myths have grown up about it. The most extraordinary is that the British fought against great odds. True, if you measure only by the numbers. The Armada that sailed against England in 1588 was 130 ships. Floating fortresses, the ships carried a total of 2,500 guns and 30,000 men, two thirds of them soldiers. Against them Queen Elizabeth I could send only 34 warships, plus scores of privately owned vessels, half of them too small to be of any value.

But look behind the numbers. Spanish galleons were unwieldy and overmasted. They often drifted in high winds because of their flat bottoms. Most of their guns were heavy, short-range cannons. They had only a few culverins—long guns with a range of over a mile. The Spanish commander, the Duke of Medina Sidonia, believed in the age-old way to fight. That was to grapple the enemy ships, board them, and unloose your soldiers for hand-to-hand fighting with the enemy.

But one of the British navy chiefs, Sir John Hawkins, had ships with far more big guns than small ones. And he had developed a revolutionary theory for their use. Do not fire cannon just for an opening salvo. No, get your fleet within range for your big guns and then batter the enemy with steady cannonading. His sailors were far better trained than the Spaniards in seamanship and fighting. In a desperate eight-hour battle in the English

Channel the British won a major victory. No English ships were sunk or captured and only about 40 seamen were killed. But because the English ran out of ammunition, two thirds of the Spanish fleet escaped.

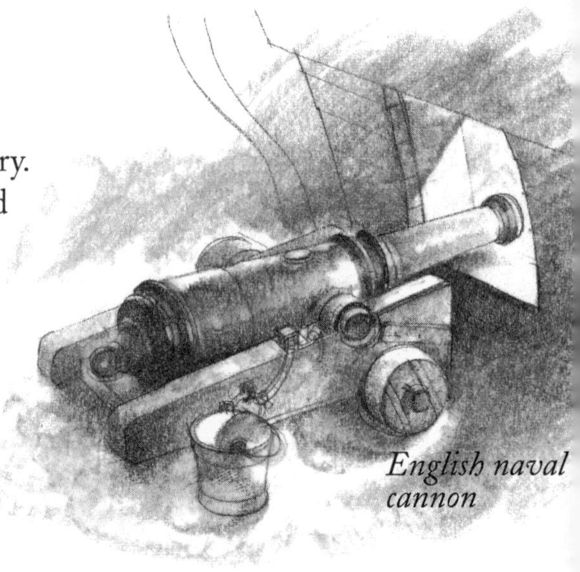

English naval cannon

Badly damaged by the English guns, the surviving Armada headed for home, only to suffer terrible hardships and losses on the way. Thousands of men died, partly due to storms, but even more succumbed to starvation and thirst. Of the 130 ships that sailed from Spain, 63 were known to be lost. The English captured or sank about 15, and 19 more were wrecked on the Scottish or Irish coasts. What happened to the remainder, no one knows.

Spain's military reputation was ruined, and the sad fate of its fleet marked a turning point in naval warfare. The old ram-and-board tactics of the galleys was dead. Heavy artillery on sailing ships with line-ahead tactics was now supreme.

Spain's king had poured a dozen princely fortunes into the Armada, and he lost the whole gamble. Now Spain's archrivals—France, the Netherlands, and England—began to make rapid gains in power.

42 *Close to Land*

For the most part navies did not operate on their own. They functioned as partners of armies on land. Sea and land forces worked out their maneuvers in support of one another. Even when the big-gun sailing ships ruled the seas, from the 1500s onward, most naval battles took place in coastal waters, very close to land. And when sail gave way to steam power, the steam warships burned coal at such a huge rate that they could not move too far from their coaling stations. So again, most naval encounters took place near coasts. That still held true in both World War I and II.

Despite the great advances in modern technology that improved communications—radio, radar, shipborne aircraft, patrol submarines—navies stay close to land. The basic reason for this is the vastness of oceans. About seventy percent of the globe's surface is covered by water. Navies continue to fight their enemies in but a tiny part of that immense area.

43 *A Small-Town Boy*

It was a small-town boy from New England who revolutionized the production of guns. Eli Whitney (1765–1825) mastered the use of tools working on his father's farm in Westboro, Massachusetts. He was a blacksmith in his youth, a nail maker on a machine he made at home, and the first maker of women's hatpins.

At twenty-three he decided to enter Yale, and after acquiring his degree, he got a job as a tutor on a cotton plantation in Georgia. Seeing how hard and time-consuming it was to separate the seeds from the fiber of short-staple cotton, within ten days he invented a machine to do it rapidly and efficiently. His cotton gin allowed one man to do the work of fifty. Almost overnight the gin made cotton production economically sound.

Nothing in the South was ever the same again. One unforeseen effect was to extend the slave system by providing the South with a new commercial crop and the world with relatively cheap cotton.

While many things conspired to deprive Whitney of the great profits he expected from the cotton gin, it didn't stifle his inventive genius. He knew that the young American nation was terribly short of skilled labor. What he did was to develop a system of manufacturing—identical replaceable parts—that allowed an unskilled person to turn out a product that was just as good as one made by a highly trained machinist.

This was soon after the Americans had won their independence from Britain. Who knew when another war might come, for which weapons in mass supply would be needed? So although he had never made a firearm before, Whitney decided to test his new system on the manufacture of rifles.

Whitney had no factory, no machines, and no capital. But his prestige as the inventor of the cotton gin persuaded the government to give him an order for 10,000 muskets to be delivered within two years.

Before this, the making of firearms was done entirely by skilled hand labor. But the parts of one gun did not fit any other gun. Whitney proposed to make all the machined parts of a musket so nearly identical that the parts could be interchangeable from one gun to another. It was a revolutionary innovation, one that could be applied to the manufacturing of many products with interchangeable parts.

Whitney did not invent the idea of interchangeable parts, but perfected a plan for carrying out what men in both England and France had thought of before him. Actually, it was Thomas Jefferson, himself a man of great inventive talent, who picked up the idea in France and suggested it for use in America.

This time Whitney made money from his innovation. He got more contracts for his arms factory from both the federal government and various states. He developed the milling machine, and his factory was the first to use power-driven tools such as the drill press. He had fulfilled the pressing need for someone to design sets of machinery for making machines, so that a factory could produce such a machine as a gun—or a clock, or a sewing machine, or an automobile, or an airplane. . . . It was the basis for all future mass production, worldwide.

44 *Like Water from a Hose*

The idea of creating a repeater gun had long intrigued inventors. They knew that a soldier armed with a one-shot gun was in bad trouble if he missed his first shot at an enemy less than a hundred yards away. The enemy with his weapon would be upon him before he finished reloading. So why not figure out a way to make a gun that would squirt out bullets like water from a hose?

As early as the 1300s inventors had tried to increase the firepower of an individual gun by stacking many barrels in layers, each of which could be ignited almost simultaneously by one or two gunners. Such ponderous contraptions were used on a small scale for hundreds of years. But gun making at that time was a very crude and unreliable craft. Although inventors had visions of what might be done to achieve a machine gun, they lacked the technological expertise to translate their theories into reality.

It wasn't until the American Civil War—the first truly modern war—that workable machine guns appeared. By 1860 the United States was second only to Britain in mechanical skills and production capacity. And once war began, technology intensified the scope and deadliness of the struggle.

The two sides pitted everything they had against each other, including their manpower. As in Napoleon's time, soldiers became more expendable than ever before. The goal was *overkill*—that is, to find and use the mechanical power to kill as many of the enemy as possible, in battle after battle, for four long years. So it was no accident that the machine gun, the weapon of mass destruction, arrived on the battlefield during this conflict.

Most of the early inventors of repeating weapons wanted to make a lot of money, win recognition, and serve their country's needs. That was true—in a strange way, as we'll see—of Richard Gatling, the first man to make a practical machine gun.

Gatling was from North Carolina, had little formal education, but had a sharp mind. He taught school and ran a country store until he found his true calling—invention. Everything seemed to interest him. He designed propellers, toilets, bicycles, farm machinery. Then, during the early days of the Civil War, an idea came to him as he watched the wounded and dead return from the front. "If I could invent a machine—a gun—that would by its rapidity of fire enable one man to do as much duty as a hundred . . . it would to a great extent supersede the necessity of large armies, and consequently exposure to battle . . . would be greatly diminished."

By 1862 Gatling had produced the first true machine gun. Its charges were fed into the chambers, fired, and extracted, all by operation of machinery. He claimed it could fire 200 rounds a minute.

Gatling wrote to President Lincoln offering his new machine gun to the Union cause, saying it was "just the thing needed to aid in crushing the present rebellion." But though Gatling had moved north to develop and promote his weapon, he had not forgotten that he was a Southerner. At the same time as he was peddling his gun to the Union, it seems he was an active member of a secret group of Confederate sympathizers, aiding the Southern cause by acts of sabotage.

The Confederates shied away from such complex weapons as the machine gun because they lacked the industrial capacity to produce either the gun or the huge quantities of ammunition needed.

If Gatling thought the North was more business-minded, he was disappointed. Both the government and the army turned him down. Still, he believed in

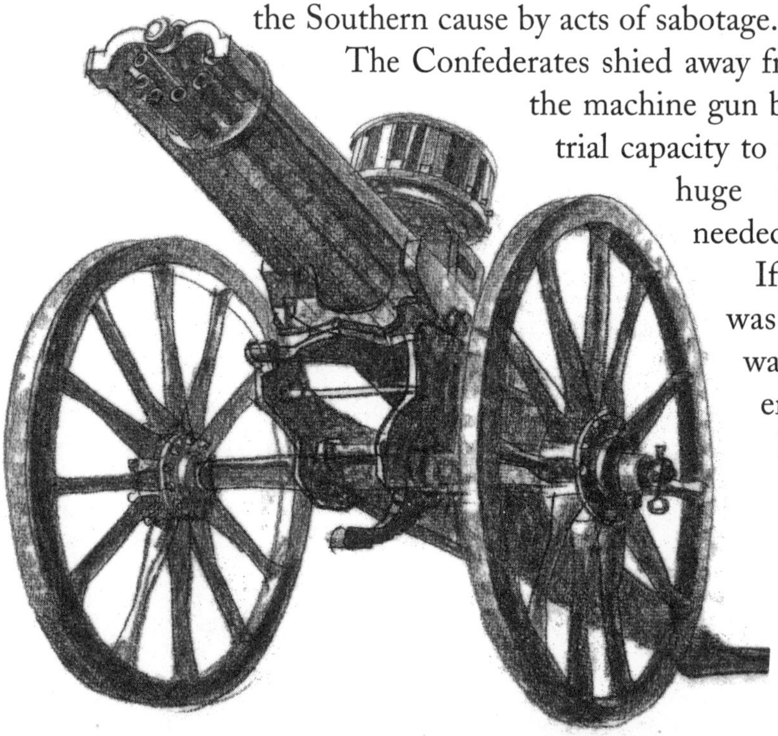

Gatling gun, 1874

his invention and scouted for foreign buyers. Through publicity he told the world that his machine gun "bears the same relation to other firearms that McCormick's reaper does to the sickle, or the sewing machine to the common needle. It will no doubt be the means of producing a great revolution in the art of warfare from the fact that a few men with it can perform the work of a regiment."

A year after the war ended, the U.S. Army adopted the Gatling gun. Soon the inventor made deals with Britain, Russia, Japan, Turkey, and Spain, usually reaping a profit of one hundred percent on every sale. As the historian of the machine gun, John Ellis, wrote: "Whilst Gatling's justification for the invention of the machine gun can to some extent be ascribed to the necessary hypocrisy of a man who stands to make money out of improving the means of killing his fellow beings, it is also significant as a classic formulation of the absolute faith men in the 19th century had in the beneficial effects of scientific, technological and industrial progress."

All the early machine guns, including Gatling's, had to be cranked by hand. The rate of fire, though fast, required a soldier to turn the handle continuously. That, said some inventors, isn't truly a machine gun. One of them, a self-educated man from Maine, decided to tackle the problem.

45 *What a Terrible Weapon*

Hiram Stevens Maxim (1840–1916) wasn't the first man to think of a weapon that would begin to fire as soon as the trigger was depressed and would keep on firing until the trigger was released. But he was the first to make that dream a practical reality. After a skimpy schooling, Maxim worked as a housepainter and wood turner, and then as a mechanic. Moving to Boston, he became

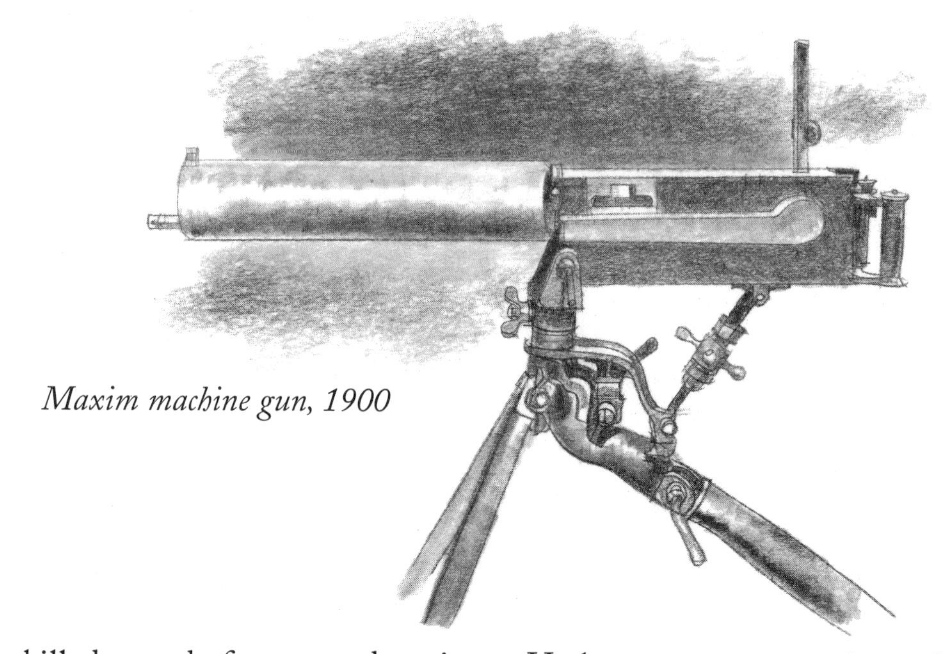
Maxim machine gun, 1900

skilled as a draftsman and engineer. He began to pour out inventions, such as an automatic repeating mousetrap, a hair-curling iron, and an automatic sprinkler system. Moving again, to New York, he invented gasoline engines and locomotive headlights as well as new chemical and electrical processes.

While in Vienna in 1882 for an industrial exhibit, he ran into a cynical American friend, who said to him: "Hang your chemistry and electricity! If you want to make a pile of money, invent something that will enable these Europeans to cut each other's throats with greater facility."

Maxim took up the challenge and spent two years in his London workshop, making drawings and building models for an automatic gun. At last he had an efficient and reliable model. The Maxim gun had a single barrel, unlike most of the crank-operated machine guns up to that time. The recoil of each shot ejected the spent cartridge and moved the next one into the chamber. The gun fired at an adjustable rate of up to 666 shots a minute.

Maxim offered his gun to the United States, but military dolts turned it down as an impractical curiosity. The British, however, were smarter; they adopted the gun. Later, Maxim developed another machine gun that operated not by recoil loading but by gas-pressure loading. One or the other of these two loading systems has been used ever since in automatic pistols and machine guns.

Later, while demonstrating his machine gun in Austria, Maxim was asked if he could solve the problem of recoil in cannons. Field guns had always been troublesome because they leaped back violently when fired, sometimes crushing a careless gunner. Maxim figured out the answer: the hydraulic recoil cylinder, soon adopted everywhere.

46 *The Price of Suicide*

The thinking of most armies lagged way behind the fundamental changes in technology brought about during the nineteenth century. Even as late as the beginning of World War I most professional soldiers still believed in rifle and bayonet as the last word in weaponry. The new machine gun threatened their old confidence in the decisive role of personal courage and individual effort in combat. What did the old virtues—fortitude, honor, patriotism—amount to in the face of a murderous barrage of bullets? Even when their governments bought machine guns, army officers ignored them. Until, that is, the First World War taught them better.

Yet in another part of the world—Africa—the officers of the European colonial powers had not hesitated to rely on the new weapon. Few in number as compared to the large native population, the Europeans used the machine gun to mow down myriads of poorly armed Africans whenever they dared to resist the theft of their ancestral lands.

What the machine gun meant in colonial Africa was put this way by John Ellis:

> In all parts of the continent, against Zulus, Dervishes, Hereros, Matabele and many other peoples . . . Maxims scythed down anyone who dared stand in the way of the imperialist advance. Such weapons were absolutely crucial in allowing the Europeans to hang on to their tiny beachheads and give themselves a breathing space for further expansion. . . . Without Hiram Maxim much of subsequent world history might have been very different.

No one, including Gatling and Maxim, wrote Ellis, "imagined what a terrible weapon they had created, how greatly they had increased man's capacity to wipe himself off the face of the earth. The imperialist experience had revealed the truth, but no one wanted to face up to it."

Yet one man did—a Polish economist, Ivan S. Bloch. In 1898, after studying military technology, he concluded that the increased firepower of modern weapons had made war impossible, "except at the price of suicide."

47 *The Agony of Loss*

Not until World War I did the machine gun finally win acceptance on all sides. Early on, only relatively few were used in action in the armies of Britain, France, and Germany. But in no time they proved what overwhelming power they gave the defense. Whichever side went on the attack could make no headway against the terrible rain of fire pouring from the often thinly held infantry positions. So each side was forced to dig deep holes in the ground for protection.

And they remained in those trenches more or less at a stalemate for four calamitous years. Just a few well-placed machine guns always wiped out attacking infantry. Casualties on a scale never experienced before in warfare horrified the people back home.

But the generals continued to shut their eyes to the significance of this new turn in warfare. "Just one more assault will do it," they kept saying. "Bring up more ammunition, more men!" And yet again another wave of young men would be sacrificed to military stupidity.

Just one engagement—the Battle of the Marne—cost each side 500,000 casualities. Before the war was over, France alone, with a population of 40 million, would lose 1,700,000 men dead and 4,500,000 wounded. On both sides, in World War I, there were at least 10 million deaths. "The casualty lists," said John Keegan, "had left gaps in almost every family circle and the agony of loss persisted for as long as those who felt it themselves survived."

48 *Tanks*

It took a new weapon—the tank—to restore the offense to what it had been before the machine gun. The idea for the tank came not from an inventor but from a British colonel. In 1914 he saw American Caterpillar tractors towing heavy artillery behind the lines. He thought, why not armor the tractor, mount guns on it, and thus overcome the power of the infantry's machine guns?

It took three years before an army made the first serious use of tanks in battle. Late in 1917 the British sent nearly 400 tanks mounted with 1,000 guns against the Germans. Still, though the tanks overcame the enemy's defense system, the Allied high command failed to use the new weapon

British World War I tank

decisively. Generals were too bogged down in the old ways for the advantage in that battle to be seized. As for the Germans, while they were the first to exploit the machine gun's potential, they missed the great potential of the tank and sent only 45 into action.

Limited by military apathy and want of imagination as the tank's use was in World War I, it would revolutionize land warfare twenty years later when World War II began.

49 *Power in the Air*

The first powered flight of an airplane took place at Kitty Hawk, North Carolina, in 1903, when the Wright brothers took to the air. But it would be several years before military commanders grasped how useful aircraft could be in war. They saw it only as a reconnaissance tool—the eyes of the ground forces.

A year into World War I, the Germans began using a fixed machine gun timed to fire through a plane's revolving propeller without hitting it. The allies copied the device from a captured German plane, and then each side began competing desperately to gain superiority in numbers of aircraft, and in their speed, firepower, and maneuverability. By 1917 a single air battle involved as many as one hundred planes.

The Germans sent bombers over Paris and London, while the British attacked the enemy's rail stations and airfields. Toward war's end the Allies' air power was much greater than Germany's. However, the planes were so small and the bombs so ineffective that air power never had the importance it would have in the next world war.

Nieuport airplane, 1917

50 *The Echo*

Enough amazing inventions and improvements came out of World War II to fill a fat volume of weaponry. To mention only some: proximity fuses, bazookas, recoilless rifles, rockets, incendiaries, fast tanks and tank destroyers, long-range fighter aircraft, armor-plated heavy bombers, carrier-based aircraft, super-battleships, antisubmarine devices, radar, and sonar. And, of course, the atomic bomb.

Almost every aspect of that war—from weapons to tactics and strategy—was influenced by scientists. The Allied forces pushed scientific achievement to its limits, while Hitler, overconfident in his own "creative genius" in devising new tactics, failed to mobilize the scientific talent of his people until it was too late. Through a huge effort, the Allies coordinated the academic and industrial scientists and the research agencies of all the armed services to work at top speed to improve old weapons, invent new ones, and develop countermeasures to lessen the power of the enemy arsenal.

The most valuable new device in the war was radar, an acronym for "*ra*dio *d*etecting *a*nd *r*anging." Based on the principle of the echo, the device could so accurately measure the time it took a radio wave to travel to an object, reflect off it, and return that the range of objects miles away could be read within yards. Radar was what saved the Royal Air Force early in the war, when Nazi planes crossed the English Channel on bombing raids. The British planes, though greatly outnumbered by the German air force, waited at their bases until the attack was launched and then were sent where needed. Aircraft losses for the Nazis were so great that Hitler gave up his plan to invade Britain.

The military with the help of scientists adapted radar to ships, plane interception, anti-aircraft guns, submarines. It was used in dozens of ways, and proved superior to optical instruments for range finding even when visibility was good. At least 150 different radar systems were produced before the war ended.

It is interesting to note that the idea for radar popped into the minds of scientists in several countries at the same time. Each research project was kept very secret, and consequently Britain, the United States, France, Germany, and Japan each developed radar systems independently.

51 *The Doomsday Weapon*

On July 16, 1945, the first experimental atomic bomb was exploded at Alamogordo, New Mexico. It was the climax of the most revolutionary military development of modern times, perhaps of all time.

It came three years after President Roosevelt had set up the secret Manhattan Project to gather the manpower and materials to carry atomic research forward. The goal was to cause a chain reaction by fission, the process by which atoms yield their explosive power. The scientists and technicians were in a frantic race to beat the Germans to the development of an atomic bomb. When the project succeeded, an Army Air Force group began secret training to prepare for dropping atomic bombs.

At the same time, a debate began among the small circle of government officials who knew about the bomb. Should this terrible weapon be used? If so, how? Would it be immoral to use such a devastating weapon? Was it even necessary, since at this late point in the war Japan was expected to collapse soon anyway?

Nonetheless, it was decided to go ahead and use the bomb. Those who made that decision believed the demonstration of the weapon would be convincing proof to the Japanese leadership of America's power to destroy the empire. If Japan went on fighting, it would mean even greater losses for their own people than for the Allies. And any last-ditch struggle could only end in defeat for them.

Atomic bomb

On August 6, 1945, an American plane dropped one atomic bomb on Hiroshima, a Japanese city of over 300,000 people. Two thirds of the city was destroyed, and 78,000 people were killed. Nearly 70,000 others were injured, and much of the remaining population suffered long-term radiation damage.

Three days later, on August 9, a second bomb exploded over Nagasaki, a city of 230,000 people. About half the city was destroyed, nearly 40,000 people were killed, and about 25,000 were injured.

The next day, August 10, Japan offered to surrender, and on August 15 the war ended.

The war ended—but the development of terrible weapons did not end. The creation of a successful hydrogen, or thermonuclear, bomb, accomplished by the United States, was demonstrated in a test in 1952. The Soviet Union achieved the same success less than a year later. Chemical weapons had been used in the form of mustard gas in World War I, and experiments with hundreds of other substances have continued in several countries up to the present. So too with bacteriological weapons. Scientists apparently cannot resist experimenting, and the military, given weapons created by new technology, cannot resist storing them, and maybe using them someday.

52 *The Human Cost*

The human cost of World War II, on all sides, was approximately 15 million military dead. Estimates of civilian deaths range between 26 and 34 million. The death toll for the Soviet Union was the heaviest—7.5 million military dead and 10 to 15 million civilian dead. Germany's loss was the second greatest: 3 million military dead and half a million civilian dead. Japan's military dead were 1.5 million, civilian dead 300,000. The United States lost 292,000 military dead, and almost no civilian dead.

53 *The Death of Life Itself?*

When the atomic bombs fell on Japan, ending World War II, they did not end fears of another, and much worse, war to come. In 1949 the world learned that the Soviet Union had exploded its own atomic bomb. In the 1950s both the Soviet Union and the United States developed a far more destructive weapon—the hydrogen, or thermonuclear, bomb. And in time their scientists learned how to marry nuclear warheads to missiles of all sizes, some with ranges of up to six thousand miles and incredible accuracy at that range.

The scientists and engineers had created a nightmare. Once upon a time tribal rivalries, national rivalries, had "acceptable" effects when it came to the outbreak of war. The harm done was limited by the power of human and animal muscle to deliver it. But new inventions and better technology down the centuries threatened greater and greater damage in war until, in the mid-twentieth century with the advent of nuclear weapons, war among nations threatened to destroy the Earth.

Thermonuclear bom

For almost fifty years Soviet–American confrontation in the "cold war" induced a dread that made peace of mind impossible. Even with the collapse of the communist system and the Soviet Union itself, that fear, while diminished, did not disappear. For while the two superpowers had agreed on measures of nuclear disarmament, too many other, smaller nations now possessed the bomb or the capacity to make it. Over the long course of human history, making war had become a habit. "Unless we unlearn the habit we have taught ourselves," writes John Keegan, "we shall not survive."

54 *A Few Facts*

In the United States:

A handgun is manufactured every 20 seconds.
A person is shot every two minutes.
A person dies from a gunshot wound every 14 minutes.
Every two hours a child dies from gunshot wounds.

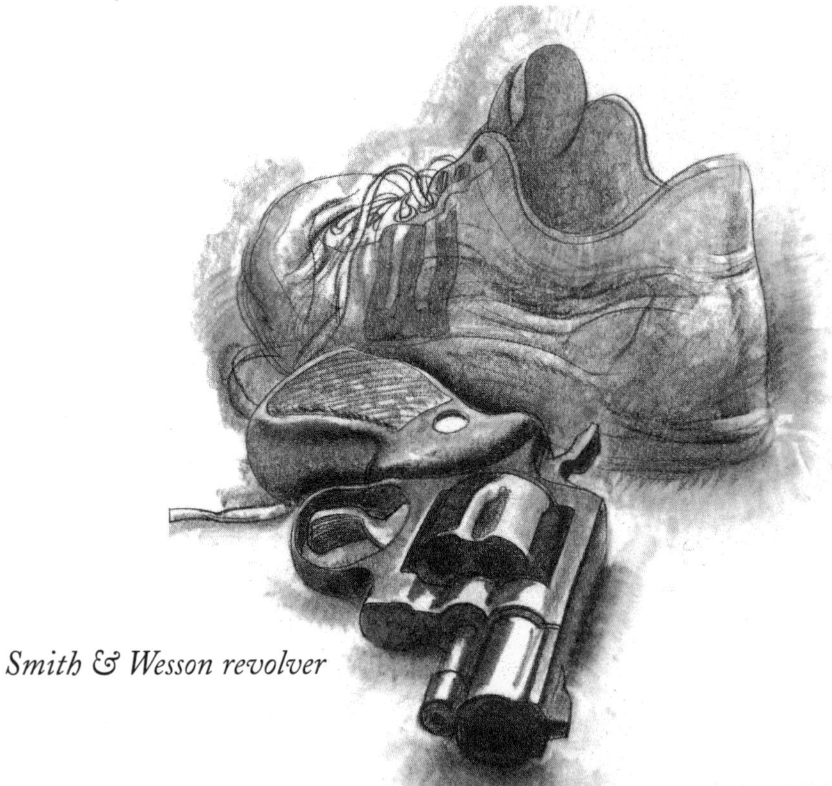

Smith & Wesson revolver

55 *Epidemic in the Streets*

Gun violence became so epidemic in the 1990s that the medical profession had to respond by developing a corps of health workers with great experience in treating gunshot wounds. The federal government reported that in 1994 about 38,000 deaths a year were being caused by guns. By comparison, it took more than a decade for 58,000 American soldiers to die in the Vietnam War. Experts estimate that injuries from guns exceeded deaths from guns by ten to one.

56 *The Profits of Death-Dealing*

In 1993 the U.S. export of weapons to countries around the world came to a total of $33 billion. That was nearly seventy percent of all weapons sold internationally—or more than the sales by all other nations put together. Unquestionably those weapons—tanks, guns, planes, bombs—wounded and killed American servicepeople as well as others. When the United States sent troops into combat in Panama, Iraq, Somalia, they faced adversaries who had received weapons or military technology from the United States.

That same year, 1993, there were 48 ethnic conflicts under way around the world. And in 39 of them, blood was being shed by U.S. weapons. A State Department human-rights report said that more than three fourths of U.S. arms sales in 1993 went to undemocratic governments.

Not only does Washington permit the sale of death-dealing weapons, it actively promotes it. The Defense Department helps American arms manufacturers to sell their products by sending staff to international arms bazaars. The United States has become "the world's leading merchant of death," said a former Assistant Secretary of Defense.

Of course the United States is not the only arms supplier. When a civil war began in Rwanda in 1990, from around the world came a steady flow of weapons—AK-47 assault rifles, long-range mortars, howitzers, and multiple-rocket launchers. Thousands died, both soldiers and civilians, and one million people were uprooted from their homes. It was "the type of market everybody wants to get in," said a Rwanda official. He added that "most countries and independent dealers that supplied the weapons were less interested in who won the war than in making money on it."

57 *Just a Way to Make Money*

Who makes the money out of guns?

A *New York Times* columnist, Bob Herbert, followed the money trail and reported his findings in December 1994. The trail led him to these manufacturers: Savage, Colt, High Standard, Marlin, Mossberg, Harrington & Richardson, Noble, Iver Johnson, Sturm, Ruger & Company, Remington Arms, and Winchester-Western.

In response to the Herbert columns, the historian William Manchester wrote that Herbert "has identified the true assassins of innocents in our schools, streets and homes . . . those for whom this domestic holocaust represents a grisly bonanza.

"To them every slain mother, every small corpse in a recess yard represents a mere profit. That *they* can live with themselves begs the question, why should we?"

Baretta, Lahti, and Walther guns

58 *Is It Natural?*

Do people kill because it comes naturally?

Or do we have to be taught to kill?

In a book about weapons and warfare the issue deserves at least some consideration.

There have been many studies of the grim psychology of the taking of human life—when it is authorized. That is, when a government or its leaders send soldiers into combat. The findings have been examined by a former Army psychologist and professor at the West Point Military Academy. Lt. Col. Dave Grossman added his own research to complete a book called *On Killing: The Psychological Cost of Learning to Kill in War and Society.*

The conclusion reached is that people, including soldiers, have a powerful natural aversion to taking human life. It seems to be a built-in taboo. Looking at the data of some wars, researchers find that as many as eighty-five percent of the soldiers did their best not to kill. They tried their hardest to get noncombat tasks, such as working on supplies, or they ran away, or, if given no choice but to face the enemy, they fired their weapons into the air. "At the decisive moment," wrote Grossman, "each man became, in his heart, a conscientious objector who could not bring himself to kill the man standing before him."

Take this fact: After the Battle of Gettysburg in the Civil War, 25,574 guns were found on the battlefield. And ninety percent were still loaded! They had not been fired. So it seems most soldiers were not trying to kill the enemy.

Then why was the casualty rate of the Civil War so high? Because the battles lasted so long that the minority of soldiers who were shooting to kill slowly took their toll.

In more recent wars, most deaths have occurred at long range—

Statue of Iwo Jima

through artillery or air bombardment. In more technologically primitive wars, it's held that the largest number of deaths occur when one side gives up and flees. The other side, in hot pursuit, finds it easier to kill from behind—when not face-to-face with the enemy. If you have to look into the eyes of the enemy, it is much harder to deny his humanity.

Soldiers (and others) become more willing to kill through advanced training methods that make killing a conditioned reflex. An example is when propaganda turns the enemy into a demon or an animal—into something less than human. Hitler trained the German people to see the Jews as vermin or bacteria, fit only to be exterminated. American propaganda used that approach against the Japanese in World War II, calling them rats and caricaturing them as beasts.

In the Vietnam War the American firing rate of weapons increased from the fifteen to twenty percent of World War II to more than ninety percent. The reason? According to the studies, through new training techniques American soldiers were "desensitized" and "conditioned" to overcome the natural resistance to killing.

59 *Does It Make Sense?*

It is hard to make sense of warfare. Suppose someone from another planet were to look down upon this Earth over the course of its history. What would that being think of religious fanatics murdering one another for the love of God? Of a nation's politicians, each desiring the best for the country, opposing each other so wildly that they plunge the nation into civil war? Of heads of state so intent on imposing their own recipes for saving the nation's soul that they starve or jail or execute myriads of their own people?

We have become so used to this miserable state of affairs that many of us do not see how stupid, how irrational, how blind has been the mass behavior of humanity.

How long will we continue to go along with such mad folly?

Bibliograpy
Index
About the Author

Bibliography

Anderson, Jervis. *Guns in American Life.* New York: Random House, 1984.

Anderson, M. S. *War and Society in Europe of the Old Regime, 1618–1701.* London: Fontana, 1988.

Brandsted, Johannes. *The Vikings.* New York: Penguin, 1965.

Brodie, Bernard, and Fawn M. Brodie. *From Crossbow to H-Bomb.* Bloomington, IN: Indiana University Press, 1973.

Bull, Stephen. *An Historical Guide to Arms and Armor.* New York: Facts on File, 1991.

DeCamp, L. Sprague. *The Heroes of American Invention.* New York: Barnes & Noble, 1993.

Dupuy, R. Ernest, and Trevor H. Dupuy. *The Harper Encyclopedia of Military History,* 4th ed. New York: HarperCollins, 1993.

Ellis, John. *The Social History of the Machine Gun.* New York: Pantheon, 1975.

Hackett, John, ed. *Warfare in the Ancient World.* New York: Facts on File, 1990.

Hogg, O.F.G. *Clubs to Cannon: Warfare and Weapons Before the Introduction of Gunpowder.* New York: Barnes & Noble, 1968.

Keegan, John. *A History of Warfare.* New York: Knopf, 1993.

Larsen, Erik. *Lethal Passage: How the Travels of a Single Handgun Expose the Roots of America's Gun Crisis.* New York: Crown, 1994.

McNeill, William H. *Pursuit of Power: Technology, Armed Force, and Society Since A.D. 1000.* Chicago: University of Chicago Press, 1982.

Mirsky, Jeanette, and Allan Nevins. *The World of Eli Whitney.* New York: Macmillan, 1952.

Oakshott, Ewart. *The Archeology of Weapons: Arms and Armor from Prehistory to the Age of Chivalry.* New York: Barnes & Noble, 1994.

Norman, A.V.P., and Don Pittinger. *English Weapons and Warfare, 449–1660.* New York: Barnes & Noble, 1992.

Slotkin, Richard. *Gunfighter Nation: The Myth of the Frontier in Twentieth-Century America.* New York: Macmillan, 1992.

Thomas, Hugh. *Conquest.* New York: Simon & Schuster, 1993.

Tunis, Edwin. *Weapons: A Pictorial History.* New York: World, 1954.

Warner, Philip. *Sieges of the Middle Ages.* New York: Barnes & Noble, 1994.

Wilson, Mitchell, *American Science and Invention.* New York: Simon & Schuster, 1954.

Index

About the Author

From his trilogy on the three kingdoms of nature—animal, mineral, and vegetable—Milton Meltzer turned to the story of how weapons and warfare have shaped human history. He has published over ninety books for young people and adults in the fields of history, biography, and social reform. He has written and edited for newspapers, magazines, radio, television, and films.

Among the many honors for his books are five nominations for the National Book Award. He has won the Christopher, Jane Addams, Carter G. Woodson, Jefferson Cup, Washington Book Guild, Olive Branch, and Golden Kite awards. Many of his books have been chosen for the honor lists of the American Library Association, the National Council of Teachers of English, the National Council for the Social Studies, and the New York Public Library's annual Books for the Teen Age.

Born in Worcester, Massachusetts, Mr. Meltzer was educated at Columbia University. He lives with his wife in New York City. They have two daughters and two grandsons.